Soul In Bloom

A Compilation of Poems

Tanushree Das

BookLeaf Publishing
India | USA | UK

Made with ❤ on the BookLeaf Publishing Platform
www.bookleafpub.in
www.bookleafpub.com

For my mother, who always believes in me.

Acknowledgements

I am truly indebted to one and all who have been instrumental in encouraging me to take up the project of getting this book of poems published. Before all others, I would like to extend my heartfelt thanks to my mother for her unflagging support. She has been the driving force, the impelling cause behind this earnest attempt of mine. Secondly, I offer my special gratitude to my publisher for publishing the poems and providing me with the fortunate opportunity to promote my work. And, last but not least, I thank my friends and colleagues from the very bottom of my heart for sincerely buoying me up when I felt low in spirits. Soul In Bloom has seen the light of day because of all of you.

Acknowledgements

Preface

I observe the world around me with eager attention, and through the poems of Soul In Bloom, I have sought to preserve the imprints of what I have gathered. I have aimed to capture a world where simplicity reigns, where life is unhurried and pure and where every breath is filled with the quiet wonder of existence. Nature to me is truly divine. She reveals the presence of infinite righteousness, infinite goodness. Within these pages, I have endeavoured to encapsulate the soft glow of her superiority – the light that brings peace and a sense of comfort. I have also written poems on the spiritual pluses of Jesus Christ and Lord Krishna. 'Your Presence' throws light on Shiva's pervasive energy. I have strived to capture the essence of bygone times as well. The stories and memories that still hang around my mind are akin to the lingering fragrance of spring. This collection of poems, in actuality, celebrates the deep and warm passion for the beauty that surrounds us, the divine that helps us navigate through the stormy waters of life, the memories pertaining to the precious moments of childhood with their comprehensively diverse aspects. Dear reader, as you read these poems, may your heart be touched by and imbued with a quiet emotional fervour.

impermanence

every joy
every sorrow
is bound to dissipate

the life she holds dear
the loveliness she prefers
everything is flying
here today
and gone tomorrow

all the wonders
of youth
and the mysteries
of dreams
are as ephemeral
as the morning mist
that vanishes
into thin air
with the rising sun

she has learnt
to live with this truth
that impermanence constitutes

the very quiddity
of existence

a magical realm

with a feeling
of amazement and admiration
I look
at the vividly coloured
flowers

they have blossomed
in such profusion
flaunting their
resplendent brilliance

dew-drops sparkle
pirouette
clinging tenderly
to the edges
of the petals

revitalising it is
indeed
this hour of the day
cool crisp
pure still
the air is perfumed

with a mellow fragrance

astounding nature

she is beckoned
to view the world anew
to recognise the subtle
and the splendid

nature's cornucopia
of wonders
astounds her
she loses herself
in her boundless grandeur
infinite energy

the peaceful green
that seems to be so fresh

and oh
this verdant ancient woodland
where life grows vigorously
in myriad forms

a young shepherdess

observe
this young shepherdess
does she not seem to be
watching something
with careful attention

seated elegantly
beneath a canopy
of tall and sturdy trees
knitting
with her deft nimble
fingers
the wool is intertwined
around them

some sheep are resting
languidly
while some are grazing
nibbling at the soft grass

she is peering
at a beauty
an array of variegated colours

a butterfly
flapping its bejewelled wings
as it sips nectar
from a wildflower

with leisurely grace

she wraps herself
in its rhythmic pattern

unruffled
by the hustle and bustle
of the outside world

soaking in
the ethereal charm

smoothly

smoothly
does the river glide
with leisurely grace

Praise Him

Praise Him
for He is all-good
He came down to the earth
for our salvation

Praise Him
for He is the giver of peace
He is the refuge and shelter
in times of difficulties

Praise Him
for He is all-knowing
He took the human form
to reveal God's love
for the world

Praise Him
for He is the shepherd
of our lot
He will lead us home
the wanderers upon whom
His undivided attention
is centred

radiance

and there
the room is brightly lit

the glow of warm lights
and warm colours
adds a warm blush
of happiness
to the space

one cannot but revel
in the sight
the colours blend
and merge
in harmonious unity
conjuring a vivid tapestry
of lively moments
both radiant and diverse

and it is as if each moment
is sublimated
by the exquisite spirit
of optimism
that permeates the air

Om Namo Bhagwate Vasudevaya

The complete incarnation
Yogeshvara
The Absolute Supreme
Yahweh Jehovah
Lord Krishna Keshava
The paragon
of strength opulence
and attractiveness
the manifestation
of knowledge infinite
O Govinda
You are the harbinger
of equanimity

born for
consolidating the path
of Prem Bhakti
for annihilating
the contrary forces of turpitude
for convoying humanity
to uprightness

for piloting man to
freedom

Srimati's
eonian companion
You cause to stream
the ambrosia
of unalloyed adherence
into the hearts
of Your votaries

You urge
Your devotees
to join the cosmic ballet
of divine play
and celestial bliss
continuing throughout
eternity

an abundance of sunlight

an abundance of sunlight
gladly beaming through trees
producing
an impressive display
of patterns and designs
lighting the path
eliminating darkness
inspiriting everything it drapes

the universe
is aware of its majesty
its attentive heart
recognises the beauty
it possesses

and she
while crossing the woods
expresses her gratitude to God
for creating those people
who weed out gloom
just like the sun's

cheerful rays

help others
see grow and survive
inspire them to prosper
and bloom

Celebration

cheers to us
cheers
to the sparkling bond
of friendship

it is time
to celebrate
our companionship
that brings with it
joy and laughter

let us sing
let us dance
may we seize
the precious instants
with illimitable
exuberance

no wonder
we are
but the breezy souls
entranced
by the magical force

of affinity

a peaceful moment

in a secluded nook
of her garden
she takes another sip
of the steaming liquid
savouring each sip
while spring's
lingering sweetness
wafts across
on the breeze

a shaft of
golden sunlight
falls on her
she feasts her eyes
on the red roses
mysteriously attractive
enchanting

a place
of quiet contemplation
a quiet celebration

her deep-seated love

for the soothing warmth
of placidity
makes her feel
de-stressed and safe

once more

once more
she enters
the lusciousness
of her scrumptious garden
bright and flamboyant
beholding the blossoms
of mesmeric hues
manifesting the exuberance
of exquisite beauty

assuaging calm
delicious peace
the mild zephyr
performing its task
of lifting her spirits

blithesome glad
she is thankful to God
eager to see
and experience
this frabjous day

pleasingly gentle

wondrously rejuvenating

everything feels right

as the moon
effloresces tonight
in the nocturnal sky
emitting beams
soft and cherished
furnishing the sphere
with its silvery hue

everything feels right
each thing seems fine
this world
is pleased and snug
grooving
on the lustrous
balmy glints

smoothly sliding
nonchalantly cruising
like a free-flowing river
wearing a gratified
expression

affably alive
beatifically blissful
contentedly composed

breathing
a gentle-divine aroma
filled with good cheer

Dhruva

fear could not
frighten him
turbulence could not
vex him
plucky Dhruva
immersed
in his thought
of reaching fulfilment
went in a
forest deep

how could he gladden
the Lord
how could he receive
His blessings

ah Narada
you came
like a glittering star
and taught him
the mantra

Dhruva began

his penance
he concentrated
his mind
on Vishnu's image
there was no alarm
on his visage

I was surprised
astonished
amazed

the earth
suddenly looked brilliant
after six months
of penance
with the glowing presence
of Vishnu's splendour
the Lord said to Dhruva
you will remain close
to the divine
if this be your desire

brightly
will you shine in the
night sky
guiding the lost

steadfast
true
you will be known
as Dhruvatara too

heaven celebrated
birds sang
rivers rejoiced
cedars danced
the luminous cosmos
extolled the triumph
of divinity
Dhruva
when accomplished
his glorious victory
Dhruva
when climbed
to the summit of glory

those halcyon days

do you remember
the days of yore
when we would sit
at the piano
for practising
playing music on it

wholly swayed
by melodies
we spent
our leisure hours
rehearsing very-many
dulcet exercises
to enhance
our sense of rhythm
to ameliorate
the flexibility
of our fingers

what's more within
a short span of time
we to our surprise
became quite adept

at playing
the instrument

even tried our hand
at playing
the canorous sonatas
of Mozart
and Beethoven

I smile to myself
when every so often
my thoughts
hark back
to those halcyon days
the days
imbued with
childhood innocence

a feeling of serenity
permeates
I ease into silence
verna's
cadenced whispers
your
attentive demeanour
the dreamy melodic strains

pertaining to
yesteryear
keep on spellbinding me

engrossed

she surrounds herself
with the shimmering quiet
of shiny elegance

engrossed
in one of her
chosen books
beguiling as it is
she peruses the grandiose
flourish of spunk
laid in it
the marvels of
thrill and zeal

what descriptions
there are
fascinate her
she is in every way
stirred up
and quite instinctively
acceding to her
absolute inquisitiveness
relating to these accounts

cruises with the characters
realising her growing
propinquity with them

recognising
the multifariousness
of the spurt of life
with fervour full
living the shaping up
of dreams and
felicitousness
alive
to the verisimilitudes
of cryptic conundrums
turning points
and afflictions
exulting in sweet-flavoured
humour
perceiving the emotions
of benevolence
and gratitude
the transcendence
of courtliness as well

she swirls
gracefully she swirls

through the billows
of words
whirls in the midst
of the antithetical notions
of happiness and low spirits
mystery and exegesis
safeness and peril

enfolding their echoes
their deep, silent
reverberations

Nature's gifts

graciously does Nature
offer her gifts
exhibiting her true love
for us

and we taste her beauty
admire the winsomeness
of her breathtaking sway
impressive as usual
noble as always
engage with her vibrancy
bathed in the glow
of a profound liveliness

content ourselves
with unruffled beatitude
bright greens, regal purples
delicate pinks, soothing blues

she pours from her heart
all the sweetness
eye-catching spectacles
amalgamating

intensity with integrity

spellbound
intrigued
full of wonder
we witness
the ethereal razzle-dazzle
Excellence paints
in striking pastels
eagerly
extravagantly
on this newly-unfurled
day's canvas

hands that take care of

what a great variety
of roses
they have in their garden
lively and happy
bouncy and bubbly
mirroring the sisters'
heartfelt devotion

both the sisters
are ardent gardeners
committed to their task
of looking after
their floral haven
they put their
hearts and souls
into acts of care
raising their earnest efforts
into a sacred service

they give
most of their time
to care for and protect
their verdant paradise

aye it is not just
a passage of hours
but a joyous celebration
of nature's eminence

their delicate touch
brings about
a calm blend of peace
and colours
provides the garden's
transient phase
a vivid splash of brightness

invitation

on a bright, clear morning
she arrives
at one of her favourite retreats
a harbour
where boats are found
to be resting patiently

she sits
at the water's edge
the sky above
a vast expanse of silken azure
spreads out
in an endless manner

a figure of quiet poise
she adorned
in a white flowing gown
dives deep
not into the sea
but into another depth

she is invited
to wander through

the vast realm of words

succumbs
to the irresistible urge
to read
embraces the worlds
of thought and illumination
where the profound
meets the beautiful

reading replenishes her
fills the vacant spaces
of her mind
nourishes the deepest roots
of her soul
without a doubt

consumed with desire
she delights in
satisfying herself
with the sparkling
pearls of wisdom
hidden within the pages
of books

benevolence

they are
a family of three
quite satisfied
with whatever
limited means they have

they may not be rich
in the most literal sense
but their hearts
are full of richness

even the little girl exudes
the warmth of compassion
ever ready to help others
who are less fortunate
than them
who are in deep agony
in acute pain

this year
they have decided
to feed those
who are homeless

starved and malnourished
and for this purpose
they have bought fish
together with bread
to prepare a special dish

to tell the truth
they will not use
all the ingredients
as others use

the spices
will be somewhat different
a little bit distinct

no artificial flavours
will be added
but rather
they will make use
of the condiments
of love and kindness
and devotion
their own spice mixes
to prepare this foodstuff

perhaps

it will be their
appropriate offering
to the Lord in disguise

gratitude

she espies the horizon
the twilight firmament
tenderly touches
the earth
with its cordial light
producing an aura
of delicacy
eliciting an impression
of amazement

yet another chance
she gets
of hailing the fruition
of a sunny day

feels once again
she has to hold onto
gratitude
for the munificence
Magnificence is bestowing
in abundance
thereby giving sustenance
and life

to all living creatures

rich in mercy
healing us with beauty
a gentle reminder
that at the core
of a pleasant life
lies both divinity
and grace

flourish unhindered

flourish unhindered
in the beauty of each day
where your thoughts may turn
to the joyous cadence
bringing together
the heavens and the earth
and soak up
energy as well as ardour
from the brilliant display
of scenes
profusion exhibits

while the Lord of Lords dances
dances
the dance of eternity

enjoy the day's glory to the full
having a close bond
with impressive motions
keeping your
ascending spirit alive
rivers are flowing ceaselessly
to mitigate your thirst

and your soul
infinitely pure sparkles
look at its perpetual light
warm yourself in its shine

while the Lord of Lords dances
dances
the dance of eternity

her small plot of paradise

she is standing
amidst the serene beauty
of her garden
all her hard labour
has at last
come to fruition

the blooms
they are delighting
in the sun's pleasant warmth
in the pleasant breeze
of spring

their soft petals
their flamboyant colours
they do proclaim
nature's charm and glory

she is savouring
every moment
relishing the etherealness

of lilies daisies
violas pansies

and I can well decipher
she has arrived
at the awareness
of a deep sense
of contentment
magnificence spreads over
her small plot of paradise

a season of simplicity

it's a beautiful display
of nature's cyclical character
gone
gone is the frozen chill
of winter
the earth stirs
from its overlong slumber

the air
alive with melodies of birds
squirrels dart rats scurry
they love to frolic
beneath the sun

joy is found
in the smallest things
in the flutter of wings
in the running of rills
in the playful chase
across the fields
and the trees
with branches bare
still they hold the promise

of sprouting leaves

this is spring
laden with simplicity
glutted with innocence
as tender as the laughter
of children
unblemished
untarnished

do allow yourself

do allow yourself
to plunge
into your own inner self
where you can taste
the nectar of immaculacy

where you can
swathe yourself with
freedom's sublime traits
sweet and satisfying

forge a sacred tie
with the most sacred pneuma
of yours
so its light may unveil
the way to peace
and joy

she needs a break

today
she is not exhibiting
any urgency to top off
her incomplete assignments

releases herself
from the clutches of duties
and responsibilities
her dreams
and aspirations
keeps at bay
the fast-moving world
and slows down

she needs a break
and rightly so
gives leave to her mind
to freely wander

the lush green lawn
those sky-touching trees
meticulously
she listens

to the music of the wind

a ripple of mirth
passes
drinks in the lustre
visible in the expressions
of children at play

the day is so unburdened
fair
holding on an evident allure
she truly acknowledges

the jewels of spring

she has taken a seat
on a tree branch
a few of her companions
are gathering flowers
and others
are engaged
in a good chinwag
their faithful dog too
partakes in
the blissful fete of life

‘Cherry blossom
cherry blossom
it's the air
that we breathe’

how they take pleasure
in viewing the flowers
the wisps of beauty
the jewels of spring
steeped in the nature
of evanescence

A quotation from Haelos has been incorporated into the poem.

intimacy

I am sure you know
you belong
to the cosmic marvel
and I am also sure
you know
in the depths of your heart
who you are intimate with

so leave
this starless night my dear
and be familiar
with your own
inner stillness
that imparts grace to you
and binds you with your spark

where your sunshine-filled world
reflects bliss
of the most pristine kind
where the waves
of transcendental energy
which make you live and breathe
are flowing uninterruptedly

their celestial rhythms
desperate to liberate you
from the fetters of gloom
encouraging you
to realise
that life is not to be
lived in darkness

instead
you must have the satisfaction
of knowing your own truth

the truth that love
and beatitude
perfume your
own pellucid soul

The poem has been based on the teachings of Mooji.

enchantment

whenever your eyes
rest upon exquisite blossoms
you perceive their gentleness
take note of the divine spark
bestrewn upon their faces
feel their captivating nature
touching your spirit
filling you
with a serene gratification

their velvety softness
sweetly perfumed breaths
in hues so vivid
speak of a sprightly quality

a paradisiacal perfection
an optimistic revelation
of the existence
of an untainted appeal

ethereality
generates a cordial milieu
an ambience

assuring the presence
of enchantment

Your presence

I have drowned myself
in the silence of infinity
the eternal mystery
caresses my existence
indicating Your presence

my whole self throbs
and thrums
a robust feeling
arises from within my heart
the entire order
encompasses You
Lord, I plead
You consign to the flames
all its impurities

You are playing damaru
I am breathing Your elegance
I clasp to this faith
You will revivify me
with the beauty
of Your essence

Your prowess exhilarates me
Your vigour contents me
I perceive
a wondrous spectacle
as I fly through the skies
of zeal
the universe moving lithely
with swaying speed
to the beat of drum

fine and pleasing

fine and pleasing
the sun comes out
brings back to freshness
the earth
it gussies itself up
in a gentle sheen
blessed favoured
defines anew
the shimmer of rejuvenation

gladly, she accepts
the warming shine
pleased relieved
her enlivened self
embraces the first blush
responsive to the morn's
rosy elegance
she offers her renewed
gratitude

compassion

after completing her task
of mending clothes
she observes her daughter

her act of feeding
hungry chickens with bread
corn rice and water
may appear small
but it contrives
a magical effect

touches lives
with the redolence
of compassion
resonates
with the quintessence
of solicitude

an intriguing radiance
a riveting glow all around
transmuting
the melancholic shroud
of gloom

into a tender cascade
of fulfilment

an ardent painter

he frequently
draws encouragement
from the varied aspects
of nature
finds peace and solace
when he is thoroughly
absorbed
in its influence

an ardent painter
he is passionate about
portraying
expansive landscapes
the themes
of his depictions
keenly establish his
proclivity
for the great outdoors
opts for scenes
that explicate
diverse impressions

in a perfect manner
he delineates
what he beholds
reveres
the divinity of nature
believes
it should be appreciated

my sacred star

holy dear I am
savouring the delectable
aroma of your benignity
the iridescence of your nobility
flowing with ease
and dynamism
like a circumfluous river
you put a novel bloom
in life

I have dived into
the numinous depths of yours
I am cherishing
its prismatic hues
the lustrous traits
of hope and peace
which you mirror

effulgence belongs to you
bliss accompanies you
the gentlest of spirits
you are
my sacred star

I go into a trance
when I see you join
the blossoms of happiness
on the harmonious string
of love

love

love
a force so radiant
spreads amusement
scatters joy
in sparkling rills
swamps the world
with dreams evergreen
soothes the heart
and scars it heals

love
more delicate than
tulip blooms
yet heftier than time
so good
shines with a sober light
guides us from disorder
to what's right

love
ripe in beauty
renews the soul
reveals constancy

makes us whole
trust patience hope
take their stance
woven together
in your gentle glance

and I am wide awake
besotted
listening to love's
ancient melody
a scarlet rose
sings for the earth

Silence

silence luminous
free from jar
free from rancour
free from fear
free from fracas
free from bemusement
free from resentment
is wearing
an enchanting smile
a smile which eases malaise
a smile which knows
no confrontation
a smile which promises
a feeling of affinity
a smile which gives out
a wondrous sheen
of clemency
a smile which conjures up
the magic of harmony
a smile which touches
my soul
and fortifies me
with its sweet-tasting
crystalline calm

the bird of paradise

you have appeared
before me magnanimously
the bird of paradise
I am looking upon you
with awe
how you take delight
in permeating
magnificence as well as
charm

the soft beams
which you emit
cast an amiable pleasure
upon my heart
your sacred majesty
imbued with healing worth
lights the dust
I sense it
from your shimmering
existence
flows oceans of energy
and the sovereignty
all your own

wrapped in the spirit
of sacrosanctity
and constantly yenning for
nourishing the sphere
with the elixir of life
you manifest
the charisma of peace
never will you give in
to chaos
knowing that beauty and love
will ultimately reign over
the world
my bird divine
rise high with royal brio
let me rejoice
in the treasures of lambent joy
cascading down
the wild blue yonder

a land full of amazements

fatigued by drudgeries
complications
and challenges
at last, he finds himself
in dixie's land
a land full of amazements

elegance is reverberating
through the milieu
he sets store
on its influence
at a leisurely pace
cherishes
the undiluted smell of freedom
the silken-soft feel of grass

incantations
the bright atmosphere
is sending out
in a gliding manner
the whole mix of cheeriness

seraphic marigolds violets roses
peonies and dahlias
uplifting heavenly
are infusing their spirit
into his heart

stunned he is left stunned
after his surveillance
their propensity for watching
cordially his every gesture

so how can he not be
fascinated by the carefully
choreographed image
of elegance
how can he not become
full of with a desire to linger here
where time stands still
and beauty overwhelms

it forever beams

she appreciates
its flowered beauty
festoons herself
with the auspicious ornaments
of its felicity
nourishes enlivens herself
with its modest sonatas
detects to her delectation
its lucency
to be so persuasive
and mesmeric to the soul
that feels its presence
its soft ecstatic radiance
the flourish of conviviality

when love halcyon beams
it forever beams
garbed in tranquil peace
unwavering fealty
sanctifying strength
informing
the pink cosmos' denizens
of the ever-growing tenderness

while flowing gently
ever so gently

rest

she gazes
at the dynamic stream
drifting seamlessly
radiating many-hued colours

the crimson flowers
odiferous
they are giving off
reams and beams
of happiness
the clear skies too
are luxuriating
in the flavour
of delicious blue

the ambience
is so blissful and sublime
heightened with
gleaming vibrancies
whilst she dwelling within
nature's breath
dreams about
instituting

an affinity with her
pleasant vibes
bent on calming
the restless stirrings
that rise within
and rest

rest amid
psychedelic nature's
adored gifting

life

life brilliantly unique
splendid spirited
full of movement
has been flowing
for keeps

and you
indissolubly attached
to your feelings
to maintain your life
of grace bit by bit
follow its subtleties
fascinated
with its sanctity
life's divine forces
which steer humane actions

life unfailingly strong
noble sublime
full of opulence
is supremely active
all the time

and you
endued with its energy
breathing its patterns
its abundance catholicity
and variegatedness
find your existence
firmly rooted in life

the letter

she is thoroughly
absorbed
hearkening
to each and every word
of the letter
being read
by her compeer

she has received
this missive
from her boon companion
after ages
who lives
in a faraway land
thousands of miles apart

she has written
about her passions
her emotions
her reminiscences
of the days in school
and college
remembrances

of the bygone times
their traits their habits

as a matter of fact
this note unfurls
the magic of friendship
its mellow breath
its magnificent capacity
its bliss and sublimity

she grooves
on the idea
that they will still
find contentment
in this solicitous relationship
which
according to many
exhibited the majesty
of sparkling harmony

will luminesce
with the same enthusiasm
just as before

This poem has been inspired by the sentiments
of 'Chitthi aayi hai' – a popular song from the 1986
Bollywood movie, and 'Purano shei diner kotha'–
a song written by Rabindranath Tagore.

explore

o dreamers
of this earth
do not be given to
despair
and keep yourselves
confined
within the lacklustre
walls of hopelessness
recognise know feel
the joy of holding onto
tantalising enchantments
glinting in the meadow
of silk-decked spectacles

dainty asters
convivial exquisite
persuading us to rise
pursue and drink
like butterflies
their nectarous innocence
encouraging us
to explore the height
of spirited existence

inspiring us
to dwell upon
wondrous moments
of astounding glaze
surprising delights
entreating us
to smoothly go along
with the life-stream
emanating warm bright
felicitous vibrations
of enthusiastic intensity

beloved grace

she wishes to be
the fountain of liveliness
beloved Grace
arrayed in the robe of
celestial glory
desirous of gliding
with life's spontaneity
alights from the winged chariot
of resplendence

life achieves a new fervour
a fresh cadence
when she regales
the withered
and devitalised souls
with her sweet-gentle melodies
her love for life is sincere
her love for life is intense

her life resembles
the life of a saint
as she sows the seeds
of wisdom and intelligence

she is ever eager
to spread the rays
of optimism
she is ever eager
to make humanity realise
that the world is the seat
of sanctified peace

chanting various delightful chants
an ethereal nymph she is
beloved Grace
streaming with grace
dreams of her immortality
whilst she walks through life
into the bower
of perennial devotion

she leans on her belief

she enters
a protective sheath
wrapped in stillness
hungers for freedom
from oppressive emotions

will she ever
grow out of this phase

desperate for
emerging in her
unfurling glory
by rising above
the petty concerns
that hold her back

she leans on her belief
in something greater
that will fortify her
help her
move forward
towards the fruition
of her fervent desire

awaiting the triumph
the fulfilment

an exotic blossom

on the move
I have come across
an exotic blossom
dappled with love's wonders

lynx-eyed
I am feasting
on the sparks
of consecrated mettle
she swathes herself with

the waves of divinity
are rising high
their succulent aroma
proliferating
over the vast expanse
of the resurrected orb

therein lies
the prospect of golden peace
therefrom arises the dream
of journeying towards
faith hope and transcendence

the dream of regenerating
one's self
with the varied shades
of benevolence

and an intense longing manifests

I wish to goodness
that our true selves
effloresce
with love's wonders

she has arrived

they have waited
for her for long
and now that
she has arrived
they know that
they have endless time
endless topics
to converse about
can talk for hours
about their tastes
inclinations preferences
predilections

the time they spend
with one another
is not a waste
they spill out their thoughts
that remind us
of the wonders of life
the marvels of friendship

the ambience
gives off

the shimmer of optimism
and we are encouraged
to find contentment
in simple things
to view things
with pleasure
and cheery courage

truly
there is something
angelic about them
the impact of their smiles
radiant and innocent
is restorative

flowing

she is flowing avidly
without cessation
and as she cannot be confined
we are keen on reflecting
on her enthusiastic movements
that help her move forward

satisfied with being dynamic
spirited enough
creates for herself her own path
by overcoming all the challenges
by crushing all the barriers
posing a threat to her

thus
she keeps going
flowing by parks herbage
heaths and moors
accompanied by blooms
of differing hues
untroubled by uncertainties
unperturbed by difficulties
babbling rippling

expanding growing
widening in course

and while she is resolute
in using her best endeavours
ferries life to every corner
trusting she will reach
in due time
her longed-for goal

at times

at times
she gives leave to her mind
to focus on the delicate
vigour of a river

perpetually gliding
pure and pristine
ever prepared
to acquiesce
itself to the bosom
of the sea
evermore an exemplification
of consecration
how she loves
to visualise in her mind
its inexhaustible flow of waters
their sweet ripples

little by little
she ferrets out
a close kinship with it
she takes in
that the same is true

of her life
what we forget to remember
is now revealed
through her perspicacity

the manifestation
must have come
as an enlightenment
that complete submission
complete giving in
to the presence divine
makes one's life fulfilled

together they move

it is like a spangle
from the auld lang syne

they have ridden
to that familiar park
in a horse-drawn carriage
the park still the same
as it was many moons back

once they savoured
sitting on
the luxuriant grass
beneath the sky
studded
with the twinkling jewels
of heaven
at the cessation of day

their hearts
were full of
love's shimmering brightness
their romance
knew no bounds
and finally, the day came

when they disclosed
their tender feelings
unveiling their hearts
to each other

now time
oh time has etched
its indelible marks
on their faces
it has taken away from them
their youthful vigour
but the dreams they spun
have not yet faded

as a matter of fact
they have developed
into a yearning more profound
a love more keen
a love more reciprocal

the curtain lifts
together they move
on the waves of faith
their love for each other
deepening

strengthening for sure

soul o soul

soul o soul
do prevent yourself
from continuing
on your swift pursuance
towards your goal

stop being perturbed
stop being rash
allow yourself
a breathing space
where you can soak up
the calm and quiet
glimpses of truth

appreciate life
dancing the dance
of love divine
its open arms
embracing trees streams
flowers

watch its every movement
ah so facile and effortless

indicial of elegance
unravelling the knots
of glowing love
floretting blazing amusing
totally splendiferous

ergo
wait for a while
restore your peace
hold on for a time
and revive your faith
quieten your mind
and notice

notice o soul
the illimitable energy
of gracious harmony
sustaining the air of bliss

that day

that day
I stepped into the prayer hall
of a cathedral
the ambience
was absolutely serene
the candles placed before the altar
gave off light brightly
and the incense sticks
they released a fragrant odour
people knelt
in quiet devotion
their entreaties they offered
before the Cross
Mother Mary, an eternal symbol
of purity and kindness
stood holding infant Jesus
to her chest

outside
the gate of the church knelt
a disabled pauper
hands stretched out
in a supplicatory prayer

distressed anguished
his voice worn from beseeching
sought alms with a spirit
of capitulation
for himself
and for his sister
they had been starving for days
yet while the faithful
the devoted
prayed within
few stopped to offer
the comfort of sympathy
beyond

I stood
between the faithful
and the forsaken
wondered
where true mercy
could be found
which could steer us
securely through life's
stormy waters
in the whispered prayers
of the so-called faithful
or in the outstretched hands
of the pauper

dawn will show up

I can see sorrow
in her eyes
she is crestfallen
and worried
fazed perplexed
staring ahead
not paying attention
to anything particular
not even listening
to the dulcet tune
her son is playing
on the flute

a negative event
might have happened
the impact of which
has obliterated
her cheerful demeanour

but fear not, dear one
again, you will smile
time they say
heals all wounds

and in due course
happiness will emerge

remember
there is a light
at the end of the tunnel
dawn will show up

have you ever

have you ever felt
connected
with the delicate blush
of autumn
enfolding the world
in warm colours

have you ever noticed
how its light
touches the earth
inspiring it to seed
new hopes

have you ever
experienced a longing
to celebrate its
mellow tranquillity
inspiriting you
to live in peace
with yourself

it is a grand show
of enriching moments

standing amid
the whirl of time

she is least bothered

she is least bothered
does not seem
to have any concern
about how the colours
will unfurl
about how liveliness
may flourish
about how her dreams
will take shape
or whether she will
succeed in spreading
fragrance sweet
and luscious
whether she will blossom
to state strongly
her magnificence
her dignity and spirit

unencumbered merry
she is perfectly content
knowing full well
that when she blooms
laden with the pleasant odour

of diaphanous modesty
and turns to light
blazing airily
to support the living
and the growing
she will speak of wisdom
woven from resilience
of miracles that do not
seek to dazzle

she will simply
encourage us to realise
to recognise
the quiet power
of being absolutely
one's own true self

a sacred ritual

just as God
who is all-merciful
all-kindness
provides
abundant provisions
for the world
rain for the thirsty
sun for the blooming flowers

so also
the mother's kindness
is unfathomable
it is immeasurable like the oceans

she
consistently generous
constantly thoughtful
continually loving
whose presence
brings a soothing effect
is a reflection of divine grace
ensuring that her children
eat sip and drink properly

from the daily offering
of sustenance

thus transforming
her ordinary duty of regaling
into a sacred ritual

she wonders

quite often
she wonders how nature
carries out
all her missions
with so much ease

ever at work
she is amazed
by the spirit
that knows no pause
moving seamlessly
through nights and days

at times blooming
splendiferously
coursing with immense
enthusiasm
on occasions
revealing her fury
reminding us
of her wildness
sometimes scattering
the seeds of peace

expecting
that a world free from strife
will emerge

she excogitates
nature's passion
for conversion
perceives her
as imploring us to adapt
not be fazed
take things as they come

forge ahead

we as denizens
of the earth
know fully well
of our obligation
of promoting
her well-being
sentient
of our commission
of spreading the vibes
of goodness

do not stand still
o wanderers
forge ahead
and make this sphere
a peaceful place
where compassion
confidence
tenderness
can thrive and live

may we contemplate
her beauties

fathom
her wonders
let's be ensorcelled
fascinated
be struck with deference

is she not
behesting us
to submit ourselves
to her divine grandeur

just breathing

rejoicing
in the affluence
of refreshing solitude
in the flourish
of sapid excellence

inhaling
the sweet savour
of floral scents
the shimmer
of delicate colours

breathing
just breathing leisure
pleasure

causing a feeling
of soft-benign
enchantment

if only the time had stopped there

behold these two young girls
they are chuckling giggling
just blissed out
lost totally lost
in their world of fancy

they have ensconced
themselves on a divan
in a bright area
of their chamber
shafts of sunlight
streaming through the open window
taking pleasure in gazing
at their sweetly beaming faces
their dolls are sitting next to them
sunny in a state of happiness
consumed with satisfaction
breathing the air
of this heavenly earth

the scissors are snipping off cloth

the needles weaving threads
with diligence and skill
the beautiful light of innocence
is shining over them
they are designing outfits
for their beloved toys
school uniforms she thinks
for soon their dolls
will attend a new school

with sincere and intense vivacity
they work
adamant about accomplishing
their task at hand
causing her to relive
her childhood days
when she too indulged
in the self-same activity
of playing with dolls

if only
if only there the time had stopped
when the world seemed so happy
and cheerful
untouched by sorrows
and tribulations

when she was at peace
with herself

a birthday gift

wearied in spirit
strapped
she walks into a flower shop
takes a brief and hurried look
at the rows of roses lilies
daisies and chrysanths
fingers nudge over them
tracing their smoothness

all at once
a simple bouquet
grabs her attention
bright but demure
it is all she can pay for
an unexceptional gift
compared to
the impressive array
of presents
others will bring
pearls and diamonds
wrapped in gleaming papers

she is on tenterhooks
a feeling of incertitude

settles upon her mind
she wonders
is her friend's love so fragile
that it is limited
to expensive gifts

then her mind becomes alive
with sweet thoughts
about her friend
her soft words
her gentle demeanour
her compassionate nature
how she wipes off
the tears from her eyes
how she encourages her
to have faith
and not be discouraged

a whole new world
supportive sympathetic
opens out to her view
she fathoms
that a present of a bouquet
garbed in real love
is more than enough

as a birthday gift

a brief pause she takes

quiet
peace
calmness

what a wonderful place
to have freedom
from din and bustle
and spend one's time
with companionable
books

she settles herself
in the bright
and pleasant
comfort of an idyllic wonder
the veering sunbeams
are amusing themselves
with trees
and flowers
playing pranks
with the small waves
of the stream
on its surface green

reading is
her escape
her satisfaction
her consolation

a brief pause she takes
reflects on what
she has read so far

maintains her engagement
with each
and every word
commanding
her close attention
makes an assessment
of the situation

discerns
the moving passions
of myriad voices
derives delectations
from missives
expressive of colourful
varieties of emotions

she travels
she travels the path

of comforting stillness

appeasing
enchanting
mesmeric

her affection runs deep

she may be young
but her love for her granny
runs deep
her mind is always occupied
with the thoughts
of her friend

whenever she comes
to her room
it is full to overflowing
with her gentle laughter
it shines bright
with a buoyant energy

she talks affably
gives her granny a hand
remains by her side
ensuring that her friend
does not feel forlorn
and dejected

an adorable sweetheart
she is

in whose tender voice
stories become bright
and breezy
she reads book aloud
for her granny
pronouncing every word clearly
creating moments
of sweetness and light
in quiet afternoons

life's miracles

slowly I am walking
around a countryside
unruffled
relishing life's miracles
the blue firmament
magnificently sublime
is holding tranquillity

Benevolence
has made things
so wonderfully
a grandiosity
of effulgent images
scattered all over
waving around
an absolute spiritual essence

trees
are standing majestically
rills are going along
blissfully
flowers are flourishing
in profusion

I inhale the perfume
of delicacy
lavenders are giving off
daisies are exuding
the aroma of fervour
the redolence
of impeccability

everything is going on
in a flowing manner
I cherish
the abundance
of divine nature
enriching me ever

a wintry evening

a wintry evening
the street is shrouded
with a chilling hush
not a single soul
can be seen maundering
through it
the frozen air
pierces every limb
and trees stripped bare
stand like silent sentinels
in the cold

vacant chairs doze
before an abandoned house
its interior
bleak and lifeless
the last breath
of summer faded long back

in the quiet
the mansion seems
to murmur of lives
once lived

dreams once dreamt
bees buzzed softly
drifted lazily among
the blooms that blossomed
in the carefully
tended garden

waiting
still waiting patiently
the rooms and homestead
to ring out
with children's
laughter and merriment
believing their empty hearts
will be stirred to life afresh

with the morning light
they will wake up one more time
sparks of joy will return
to their eyes

besotted

winsome birds
beguiling
are their hymns of praise

oh how they welcome
with unwearied zest
the pleasing light
embodying a divine spark

another dawn
with its sweet flavour
charms her
as she treads
the peaceful path
besotted

the illimitable shine

every single dawn
she desires
to immerse herself
in nature's magnificence
and sip the nectar
of perfections
to give up intricacies
which do not allow her
to follow the worth
of pristine simplicity

she gives off happiness
when she looks at her
the perpetual flow of life
the strength of courage
the wisdom of balance
beauty generosity
and affluence

what a fine display
of sumptuousness
she wonders
graceful nature

all-holy all-divine
brings out
the illimitable shine
of the Eternal's splendour

after a long spell of drought

after a long spell
of drought
the earth feasts
on the soft touch
of wholesome
aqueous
nourishment
creating bliss
generating serenity
imparting ease

the rhythm
of auspiciousness
happily
murmuring
the cadence of glee
throbbing
amidst
increasing optimism

trees and leaves

glisten
the parched meadows
gleam
with droplets of life
thank God
for softening the soil
with showers

for lending exuberance
the shades of relief

our love for humanity is deep

on a lovely fine morning
as she languidly saunters
amid blooming bushy trees
amid trees breathing
in the realm of the living
she revels
in the profusive abundance
of nature's grappling sumptuousness
delves into her luxuriance

nature furnishes
with opulence
to enrich people to brace them
the most arresting to her mind
the most rejuvenating
and refreshing
she muses on the comforts
fetching nature
accords on us munificently

a very special missive

she receives
when the trees endowed
with subtle insight
gingered up
with consummate mastery
utter softly in her ears
'Our love for humanity is deep
and profound for you are
the caretakers of the earth'

the revelation is startling
spellbinding
she flabbergasted
nevertheless clear in her mind
and right in being submissive
to unstinting nature fathoms
she has an authentic responsibility
to perform

so she shields
her own little garden
of trees blossoms and buds
for this is her realm
to foster
to love

A quotation from Dianne Robbins has been incorporated into the poem.

transfixed in reverence

barefoot, she treads
the sandy path
that leads to the sea
holding a bouquet of roses
in her hand

the waves she sees
crash onto the shore
rising and falling
in timeless harmony

elegance
rolling conveniently
across each wave
moving from wave to wave
shedding a lustre
on every motion

she stands
transfixed in reverence
the sea expands
beyond her grasp
limitless

serene

but the petals
which are still blushing
with life
she knows as all blooms must
these too will fade
in their own time
a stark contrast to the sea
that stretches before her

though writhing with

though writhing
with gruesome jolts and shocks
though sepulchred
in the tomb
of ruthless murderous
cruelty

the vast sea
of human life
never gives itself
up to despondency

beseeching ever
for the unfolding
of diversely
variegated relucence
of plushy benediction

pondering upon
fleecy compassion's
beatified majesty

waiting longingly
for the dulcet strains
of soft smooth serenades
pertaining to clemency
to manifest their
glowing light
their ethereal luscious
lenience in profusion

9 789363 307766

Printed by Libri Plureos GmbH in Hamburg, Germany